YOUR KNOWLEDGE HAS VALUE

- We will publish your bachelor's and master's thesis, essays and papers

- Your own eBook and book - sold worldwide in all relevant shops

- Earn money with each sale

Upload your text at www.GRIN.com
and publish for free

Remi Bauer

Aus der Reihe: e-fellows.net stipendiaten-wissen

e-fellows.net (Hrsg.)

Band 894

Sustainability at mega-sport events in developing countries on the example of the 2010 FIFA World Cup South Africa

GRIN Publishing

Bibliographic information published by the German National Library:

The German National Library lists this publication in the National Bibliography; detailed bibliographic data are available on the Internet at http://dnb.dnb.de .

This book is copyright material and must not be copied, reproduced, transferred, distributed, leased, licensed or publicly performed or used in any way except as specifically permitted in writing by the publishers, as allowed under the terms and conditions under which it was purchased or as strictly permitted by applicable copyright law. Any unauthorized distribution or use of this text may be a direct infringement of the author s and publisher s rights and those responsible may be liable in law accordingly.

Imprint:

Copyright © 2012 GRIN Verlag, Open Publishing GmbH
Print and binding: Books on Demand GmbH, Norderstedt Germany
ISBN: 978-3-656-59649-3

This book at GRIN:

http://www.grin.com/en/e-book/268657/sustainability-at-mega-sport-events-in-developing-countries-on-the-example

GRIN - Your knowledge has value

Since its foundation in 1998, GRIN has specialized in publishing academic texts by students, college teachers and other academics as e-book and printed book. The website www.grin.com is an ideal platform for presenting term papers, final papers, scientific essays, dissertations and specialist books.

Visit us on the internet:

http://www.grin.com/

http://www.facebook.com/grincom

http://www.twitter.com/grin_com

Leeds Metropolitan University

Sustainability at mega-sport events in developing countries on the example of the 2010 FIFA World Cup South Africa

MSc International Events Management

Remi Bauer
13.01.2012

Word count – 2.995

TABLE OF CONTENTS

1. INTRODUCTION	2
2. SUSTAINABILITY	2
2.1 DEFINITION	2
2.2 SUSTAINABILITY AND MEGA-SPORT EVENTS	2
3. THEORETICAL APPROACH	3
3.1 TRIPLE BOTTOM LINE MODEL	3
3.2 PEOPLE, PLANET AND PROFIT	3
4. 2010 FIFA WORLD CUP SOUTH AFRICA	4
4.1 THE EVENT	4
4.2 TRIPLE BOTTOM LINE	4
4.2.1 PEOPLE	4
4.2.2 PLANET	6
4.2.3 PROFIT	6
4.3 CRITICAL ANALYSIS	7
5. CONCLUSION	8
6. BIBLIOGRAPHY	9

1. Introduction

With the London 2012 Olympic Games, sustainability within mega-sport events has come to attention again as the organisers of the event are seeking to create a truly green event (London2012 2009a, London2012 2009b). But not only developed nations are hosting such large-scale events. Recently, the FIFA World Cup was held in South Africa, the Commonwealth Games in India and the next Olympics will be staged in Brazil (Konrad-Adenauer-Stiftung 2011). Thus, this paper will deal with the following question. Can sustainability be achieved at mega-sport events in developing countries? The FIFA 2010 Soccer World Championships in South Africa will be used as a descriptive example of a past mega-sporting event. The goal of the paper is to answer this question while also giving a diligent insight and thorough understanding of the Triple Bottom Line Model.

2. Sustainability

To provide a deeper understanding to the core of this paper, sustainability will be defined and then put into the context of mega-sport events.

2.1 Definition

There is not one single approach to defining sustainability (Blackburn 2007). One of the most popular definitions is from the World Commission on Environment and Development (1987) and states that "sustainable development is development that meets the needs of the present without compromising the ability of future generations to meet their own needs." This characterisation has been criticised for its ambiguity (Saha 2009). Another definition delivered by Munier (2005) states that sustainable development is a combination of factors, which are economic growth, social progress as well as environmental protection. This goes hand in hand with academic literature that came to a consensus that the three key pillars of sustainability are environmental protection, economic progress and social justice (Saha 2009). Sustainability aims at enhancing all three features simultaneously (Hitchcock and Willard 2006).

2.2 Sustainability and Mega-Sport Events

When looking at the historic development of sustainable mega-sport events, one can see that it is a relatively new practice. The International Olympic Committee can be identified as initiator. In 1994, the committee acknowledged the significance of environmental issues and sustainable development (Konrad-Adenauer-Stiftung 2011). In 1999, Agenda 21 was implemented to the Olympic Movement. It states that the Olympic Movement will contribute by making sustainable development-favouring measures part of their policies and, hence, supporting the cause through sportive activities (Corral et al. 2010). Another breakthrough was in 2003, when the Olympic Games Impact Study was launched. To measure the effect of the Olympics, over 100 gauges were developed and then clustered into three scopes of sustainable development: economic, environmental and socio-cultural. The 2000 Sydney Summer Olympics were one of the first ones to feature a clear environmental agenda. The first FIFA World Cup™ with a sustainable programme on the other hand was Germany in the year 2006 (Konrad-Adenauer-Stiftung 2011). Currently, the ISO 20121 for Event Sustainability Management Systems is developed and will provide an international, voluntary guideline for all types of events to achieve sustainability (Abele and Holzbaur 2011). All in all, the spotlight is on mega-sport events as they deliver a unique environment to display symbolic politics and, hence, can be viewed as a driver for sustainability (Death 2011).

3. Theoretical Approach

Further, comprehension of the Triple Bottom Line Model is essential for understanding the essence of this paper as it is the theoretical framework on which this analysis is based. To comprehend this model, the Triple Bottom Line as a concept and then its individual features will be detailed.

3.1 Triple Bottom Line Model

The Triple Bottom Line Model focuses on social, economic and environmental outcomes (Dunphy 2000). These three pillars are also referred to as People, Planet and Profit (Henderson 2011) or the Three Es, namely Economy, Environment and social Equity (Hitchcock and Willard 2006). To achieve true sustainability, one needs financial sustainability and put it into perspective with people and planet (Henderson 2011). All three aspects have to be fulfilled at the same times. Having a trade-off violates the basic premise behind the Triple Bottom Line (Hitchcock and Willard 2008).

3.2 People, Planet and Profit

The aspect related to people deals with social factors referring to the fact that one should aim to create a strong civil society (Raj and Musgrave 2009a). The overall goal is to maximise the overall benefits whilst diminishing the negative social impact costs for the people affected (Tassiopoulos and Johnson 2009). The second part of the Triple Bottom Line model focuses on environmental issues which are mainly linked to the reduction of waste as well as stopping and reversing the negative effects of exploiting natural resources (Raj and Musgrave 2009a). Further it emphasises that the use of resources should be controlled, overconsumption restricted and natural diversity preserved (David 2009). The last component of this theory framework is of economic nature relating to the fact that it is important to maintain economic capital (Raj and Musgrave 2009a). Further, it highlights that economic growth has to be achieved by increasing the efficiency of the input and output cycle while focusing on enhancing the inflow of financial means and revenues (Raj and Musgrave 2009b). This element is important as a company needs to remain competitive (Elkington 1999).

4. 2010 FIFA World Cup South Africa

The previous chapter provided a sound explanation of sustainability and the Triple Bottom Line Model. To further illustrate this, a case study will be conducted, exemplifying how sustainability has been applied at events.

4.1 The Event

The 2010 FIFA World Cup was a large-scale event which was held from June 11th till July 11th 2010 in South Africa. Overall, 32 national football teams competed at nine different venues completing 64 games. In total, 3,178,856 attendees watched the games at the soccer stadia in the host country (Technical Study Group 2010). After the Olympic Games, the FIFA World Cup is the largest sporting event in the world (Otto and Heath 2010). In 2010, this mega-sport event was held on the African continent for the first time depicting an integration of the developing nation South Africa into the globalised world (Witt and Loots 2010). Nevertheless, the question remains whether the local government and the FIFA organising bodies could live up to their benevolent objectives of leaving a positive legacy in economic, social-ecological and environmental terms (2010 FIFA World Cup^{TM} Organising Committee South Africa 2010).

4.2 Triple Bottom Line

To evaluate in how far this event measured up to sustainable standards, it will be assessed using each aspect of the Triple Bottom Line Model.

4.2.1 People

As a positive effect on the civil society one can say that the FIFA World Cup united diverse groups of the South African society (Death 2011). Further, a decreased crime rate during the World Cup could be observed with fewer robberies, assaults on foreign visitors and murders during the period of the tournament. This can be traced back to the high police visibility (South African Police Service 2011). Another social benefit is the FIFA 2010 official campaign '20 Centres for 2010'. Its goal is to accomplish favourable social change through soccer by constructing twenty 'Football for Hope Centres' which promote public health, soccer and education across the African continent. The centres will be located in underprivileged areas and assist to develop education and health services for young individuals. Overall, the campaign will sponsor social development through sports, starting a lasting physical social legacy for Africa and its World Cup. Thus far, four centres started their operations in South Africa, Kenya, Mali and Namibia. All 20 Football for Hope Centres will be finished in the year 2012 (streetfootballworld 2011). Despite the positive social benefits mentioned in the beginning of this passage, one has to mention that the harmony and excitement demonstrated by South Africans for the duration of the international soccer tournament was a temporary stage and the World Cup legacy is more theoretical than factual. The 2010 FIFA tournament could not hold off strikes by the construction work force and the moment the football championships were ending, the cohesive effects of the World Cup had instantly vanished with the spectre of chauvinistic assaults on foreign nationals raising its head (Cottle 2010). Further, in South Africa, every tenth citizen does not have proper housing. Hence, South Africans heavily rely on subsidised housing projects. Such projects have seen major cutbacks as public monetary funds were devoted to event-related infrastructure. Additionally, the FIFA 2010 affected construction supplies and land costs to rise drastically leading to even fewer public housing being constructed. The local inhabitants were also affected by resettlement procedures as local authorities relocated housing settlements to create a more valuable landscape (Steinbrink, Haferburg and Ley 2011). Moreover, some research has shown that large sporting events have a negative effect on the majority of people in host societies. This is especially true for those who are not located at or close to the event venues. Without clear strategies, it is doubtful that mega-sport events have widespread success. In the FIFA 2010 case, it was already predicted beforehand that it might end in widely uneven benefits for South Africans (Giampiccoli and Nauright 2010). Due to its design, the World Cup benefitted those South African host cities and provinces of the event disproportionately more than the non-hosting areas of the country causing additional conflict within the developing nation. Consequently, some areas did not profit in terms of welfare and infrastructure development. Regardless of the collective positive effects of the international soccer tournament, it is the government's responsibility to guarantee equity in the distribution of benefits resulting from mega-sport event, which did not happen in the South African case (Mabugu and Mohamed 2011).

4.2.2 Planet

The 2010 FIFA World Cup dedicated itself to be green by concentrating on the following main aspects: carbon mitigation, water and energy conservation, waste management, as well as transport and mobility. Prior to the tournament it was stated that renewable energy sources such as wind farms, biogas and energy-efficient lighting will be used to provide certain needs of the Soccer World Cup. In terms of waste prevention and decreasing measures, packaging was minimised and recycling measures were put in place. Sustainable transport was adapted by relying on alternative fuels and green technologies such a biodiesel and bioethanol. Further, South African authorities emphasised the benefits of using substitutes to private car transportation (UNEP 2010). The challenge with keeping the carbon footprint of the FIFA 2010 to a minimum is, that more than 65% is caused by intercontinental travel, where spectators do not have any alternative choices to air travel for long distances. An additional 17% result from inter-city transport, where also few options are offered in South Africa. Furthermore, South Africa is a more greenhouse gas intensive economy than previous host countries such as Germany which consequently results in increased carbon dioxide emissions (Econ Pöyry 2009). Overall, the mega-event caused the biggest carbon footprint any FIFA contest has ever seen (Cornelissen, Bob and Swart 2011). Moreover, a study by Greg McManus has estimated that the increased number of international visitors is likely to consume an extra amount of "2.50 billion litres of water and 420,000 megawatts of power and create almost 23,000 tonnes of waste in just fourteen days" (Otto and Heath 2010). While the larger host metropolises implemented some environmental programmes into the event planning, the goal of applying those strategies on a long-term basis to create an ecological legacy was not realised (Cornelissen, Bob and Swart 2011). To achieve long-term environmental sustainability through the World Cup is aggravated by the FIFA, as the organisation does not seem to put great emphasis on environmental outcomes on their tournaments, and does not call for host countries to offer an agreement to achieve minimum environmental performance standards (City of Cape Town 2011). Overall, the potential that was created by the FIFA 2010 was not fulfilled at its best (Death 2011). This can be a result of the fact that South Africa did not set clear measurable targets in many aspects linked to environmental sustainability (City of Cape Town 2011).

4.2.3 Profit

Overall, the Soccer World Cup 2010 was endorsed as a catalyst for economic development by the South African government (Briedenhann 2011). Pre-event estimates stated that a revenue of R93 billion, with R19 billion in tax income are expected. Further, it was hoped that 415,000 new employment opportunities would be created. The national government bodies invested over R600 billion in the years prior to the World Cup. Yet, with only R3.64 billion, tourist spending was significantly lower than pre-event estimates predicted (Cornelissen, Bob and Swart 2011). While increased demands for vuvuzelas, tour guides and tourist-sights around arenas have been observed after the World Cup, South African industrialists appear to have been mostly unaffected by the mega-sporting event (Du Plessis and Maennig 2011). Generally, economic profits that can be traced back to the FIFA 2010 mostly benefited the economic elite. Another negative aspect is that the viability of the newly built sporting venues was not considered. Hence, the arenas are now a burden on taxpayers who have to finance the maintenance costs of the sites (Maharaj 2011). Overall, most mega-sport events are too costly for local governments to host and can cause large deficits for the hosts (Preuss 2009). Therefore, it is an ethical question, whether it is alright for governments of developing countries to invest money in mega events instead of supporting other causes. The resources could instead be used to ease existing social problems in these societies. This is especially true, as it is not sure whether the short-term as well as long-term benefits of large-scale events will be enough to cover the direct costs caused by such mega events (amilnal 2010). Deductive, it is not surprising that research puts forward that in the majority of cases mega-sport events are an even poorer monetary investment for developing countries than for industrialized nations (Matheson and Baade 2003). However, it will take about five to ten years post-Games to judge the event's economic benefit. Hence, it is still too early to draw definite conclusions about the 2010 FIFA World Cup (Economic & Social Research Council 2010).

4.3 Critical Analysis

South Africa competed to host the FIFA 2010 Soccer World Cup as they perceived that doing so will boost their international reputation and fuel their economy. However, the country would have been better off carefully assessing booster promises of monetary benefits from holding a mega-sport event before spending extensive public funds to such an event. Without a doubt, holding such a premier tournament might be more of a problem than an honour in the South African case (Matheson and Baade 2003). Yet, the FIFA 2010 in South Africa created some economic benefits. However, these positive effects only reached the privileged making the World Cup a ruling class project (Maharaj 2011). This neo-classical economic approach kept the status quo within South African society (Sherman et al. 2008). In consequence, the socio-economic imbalances in the developing country were further imbedded. As main cause for failure of mega events, the unequal connections between political representatives and industry elite on the one hand and the poor on the other hand can be pointed out (Maharaj 2011). Furthermore, in social terms, the FIFA 2010 had a negative impact on the underprivileged part of the population that relies on publically funded housing (Giampiccoli and Nauright 2010). When assessing the environmental sustainability, one has to say that there were good attempts by the host country to set a green example. However, due to the high carbon footprint, those measures seem to be more greenwashing than factual as hardly any long-term changes were achieved (Cornelissen, Bob and Swart 2011). Overall, when looking at single aspects of the Triple Bottom Line Model, one can observe that 2010 FIFA World Cup South Africa has not performed well in any category. Hence, it can be concluded that the international soccer tournament failed to be sustainable. Even when looking at the event by using the Pareto improvement, where something is considered good if at least one person is better off without worsening the situation for other individuals, one has to say that the FIFA World Cup 2010 has failed as parts of the nation was effected negatively (Callahan 2004). This review does not state that everything about the FIFA 2010 was negative as assessing effects such as nation branding and international reputation are beyond the scope of this paper. Furthermore, longer-term tracking of the most relevant indicators for sustainability is necessary to come to a clear conclusion. As this time period is suggested to be at least five to ten years post-tournament, it is too early to judge all aspects of sustainability (Economic & Social Research Council 2010). Nevertheless, one can state that the FIFA World Cup in South Africa had the potential to make a difference when it comes to sustainability; however that potential was certainly not realised due to the weak sustainability performance (Death 2011).

5. Conclusion

Concluding, one can say that the outcomes of sustainable measures are very hard to assess and that long-term tracking is necessary to do so (Collins, Jones and Munday 2009). When looking at the 2010 FIFA World Cup South Africa it is evident, that it is especially hard for developing countries to achieve sustainability as economic, social and environmental aspects have to be considered. While positive legacies can be generated, economic prospects hardly come true. From a sustainable development viewpoint, there are high costs for putting on mega-sport events, where the monetary funds could alternatively be invested in education, health or housing projects. Such measures would bring a greater overall sustainable development benefit than investments in a large-scale event (City of Cape Town 2011). "While we may not have all the answers on the appropriate approach to hosting the World Cup and other mega-events, such events clearly hold immense potential for developing countries – not only to draw the world's attention to them, but, more importantly, to encourage their environmental and social sustainability. However, exactly how this potential is to be realised needs further attention and debate" (City of Cape Town 2011).

6. Bibliography

2010 FIFA World Cup™ Organising Committee South Africa (2010) **KE NAKO. Celebrate Africa's Humanity™** [Internet]. Available from: <http://www.gcis.gov.za/resource_centre/multimedia/posters_and_brochures/brochures/sa2010_govprep.pdf> [Accessed 29 December 2011].

Abele, K. and Holzbaur, U. (2011) **Nachhaltige Events: Nachhaltiger Erfolg durch Verantwortung – Ein Leitfaden für Veranstalter, die auf eine positive Wirkung ihrer Veranstaltung im Sinner der Nachhaltigen Entwicklung Wert legen** [Internet]. Available from: <https://aalen.de/sixcms/media.php/91/nachhaltigeevents.pdf> [Accessed 03 January 2012].

amilnal (2010) Developing Countries: Hosting International Sporting Events Part 1. **Jamaican Journal** [Internet]. Available from: <http://www.jamaicanjournal.com/index.php/2010/04/30/developing-countries-hosting-international-sporting-events-part-1> [Accessed 28 December 2011].

Blackburn, W. (2007) **The Sustainability Handbook**. London, Earthscan.

Briedenhann, J. (2011) Economic and Tourism Expectations of the 2010 FIFA World Cup – A Resident Perspective. **Journal of Sport & Tourism** [Internet], 16 (1), pp. 5-32. Available from: <http://dx.doi.org/10.1080/14775085.2011.568085> [Accessed 04 November 2011].

Callahan, G. (2004) **Economics for real people: an introduction to the Austrian school.** 2nd ed. Auburn, Ludwig von Mises Institute.

City of Cape Town (2011) **2010 FIFA World Cup – Host City Cape Town: Green Goal Legacy Report** [Internet]. Available from: <http://www.capetown.gov.za/en/GreenGoal/Documents/Green_Goal_Legacy_Report%20final.pdf> [Accessed 31 December 2011].

Collins, A., Jones, C. and Munday, M. (2009) Assessing the environmental impacts of mega sporting events: Two options?. **Tourism Management** [Internet], 30 (2009), pp. 828–837. Available from: <www.elsevier.com/locate/tourman> [Accessed 07 November 2011].

Cornelissen, S., Bob, U. and Swart, K. (2011) Towards redefining the concept of legacy in relation to sport mega-events: Insights from the 2010 FIFA World Cup. **Development Southern Africa** [Internet], 28 (3), pp. 307-318. Available from: <http://dx.doi.org/10.1080/0376835X.2011.595990> [Accessed 06 October 2011].

Corral, C. et al. (2010) Principles of the Olympic Movement. **Journal of Human Sport and Exercise** [Internet], 5 (1), pp. 3-14. Available from: <http://rua.ua.es/dspace/bitstream/10045/13101/1/JHSE_5_1_2.pdf> [Accessed 03 January 2012].

Cottle, E. (2010) **A Preliminary Evaluation of the Impact of the 2010 FIFA World Cup™: South Africa** [Internet]. Available from: <http://www.sah.ch/data/D23807E0/ImpactassessmentFinalSeptember2010EddieCottle.pdf> [Accessed 28 December 2011].

David, L. (2009) Environmental Impacts of Events. In Raj, R. and Musgrave, J. eds. **Event Management and Sustainability.** Oxfordshire, CAB International, pp. 76-90.

Death, C. (2011) 'Greening' the 2010 FIFA World Cup: Environmental Sustainability and the Mega-Event in South Africa. **Journal of Environmental Policy & Planning** [Internet], 13 (2), pp. 99-117. Available from: <http://dx.doi.org/10.1080/1523908X.2011.572656> [Accessed 06 October 2011].

Du Plessis, S. and Maennig, W. (2011) The 2010 FIFA World Cup highfrequency data economics: Effects on international tourism and awareness for South Africa. **Development Southern Africa** [Internet], 28 (3), pp. 349-365. Available from: <http://dx.doi.org/10.1080/0376835X.2011.595994> [Accessed 04 November 2011].

Dunphy, D. (2000) **Sustainability: the corporate challenge of the 21st century.** Australia, Allen & Unwin.

Econ Pöyry (2009) **Feasibility Study for a Carbon Neutral 2010 FIFA World Cup in South Africa** [Internet]. Available from: <http://www.norway.org.za/NR/rdonlyres/3E6BB1B1FD2743E58F5B0BEFBAE7D958/114457/FeasibilityStudyforaCarbonNeutral2010FIFAWorldCup.pdf> [Accessed 3 January 2012].

Economic & Social Research Council (2010) **Olympic Games Impact Study – London 2012 Pre-Games Report** [Internet], London, University of East London and the Thames Gateway Institute for Sustainability. Available from: <http://www.uel.ac.uk/geo-information/documents/UEL_TGIfS_PreGames_OGI_Release.pdf> [Accessed 28 November 2011].

Elkington, J. (1999) **Cannibals With Forks – The Triple Bottom Line of the 21st Century Business.** Oxford, Capstone.

Giampiccoli, A. and Nauright, J. (2010) Problems and Prospects for Community-based Tourism in the New South Africa: The 2010 FIFA World Cup and Beyond. **African Historical Review** [Internet], 42 (1), pp. 42-62. Available from: <http://dx.doi.org/10.1080/17532523.2010.483796> [Accessed 04 November 2011].

Henderson, S. (2011) The development of competitive advantage through sustainable event management. **Worldwide Hospitality and Tourism Themes** [Internet], 3 (3), pp. 245-257. Available from: <www.emeraldinsight.com/1755-4217.htm> [Accessed 06 October 2011].

Hitchcock, D. and Willard, M. (2006) **The Business Guide to Sustainability – Practical Strategies and Tools for Organizations.** Earthscan, London.

Hitchcock, D. and Willard, M. (2008) **The Step-by-Step Guide to Sustainability Planning – How to Create and Implement Sustainability Plans in Any Business or Organization.** Earthscan, London.

Konrad-Adenauer-Stiftung (2011) **Sustainable Mega-Events in Developing Countries: Experiences and insights from Host Cities in South Africa, India and Brazil** [Internet]. Available from: <http://www.kas.de/wf/doc/kas_29583-1522-2-30.pdf?111209095524> [Accessed 03 January 2012].

London2012 (2009a) **Sustainability guidelines – corporate and public events - Second edition: May 2010** [Internet]. Available from: <http://www.london2012.com/documents/locog-publications/london-2012-sustainability-events-guidelines.pdf> [Accessed 12 November 2011].

London2012 (2009b) **Towards a one planet 2012** [Internet]. Available from: <http://www.london2012.com/documents/locog-publications/london-2012-sustainability-plan.pdf> [Accessed 12 November 2011].

Mabugu, R. and Mohamed, A. (2011) **The Economic Impacts of Government Financing of the 2010 FIFA World Cup** [Internet]. Available from: <http://www.google.com/url?sa=t&rct=j&q=&esrc=s&source=web&cd=4&ved=0CD4QFjAD&url=http%3A%2F%2Fwww.ekon.sun.ac.za%2Fwpapers%2F2008%2Fwp082008%2Fwp-08-2008.pdf&ei=Pjb7TtKVCdP18QOBh-yuAQ&usg=AFQjCNHKYqc1tCl5-xTSW8aj8x1vcT0dWg> [Accessed 28 December 2011].

Maharaj, B. (2011) 2010 FIFA World Cup^{TM}: (South) 'Africa's time has come'?. **South African Geographical Journal** [Internet], 93 (1), pp. 49-62. Available from: <http://dx.doi.org/10.1080/03736245.2011.572473> [Accessed 04 November 2011].

Matheson, V. and Baade, R. (2003). **Mega-Sporting Events in Developing Nations: Playing the Way to Prosperity?** [Internet]. Available from: <http://web.williams.edu/Economics/wp/mathesonprosperity.pdf> [Accessed 28 December 2011].

Munier, N. (2005) **Introduction to Sustainability: Road to a Better Future.** Dordrecht, Springer.

Raj, R. and Musgrave, J. (2009a) Introduction to a Conceptual Framework for Sustainable Events. In Raj, R. and Musgrave, J. eds. **Event Management and Sustainability.** Oxfordshire, CAB International, pp. 1-12.

Otto, I. and Heath, E. (2009) The Potential Contribution of the 2010 Soccer World Cup to Climate Change: An Exploratory Study among Tourism Industry Stakeholders in the Tshwane Metropole of South Africa. **Journal of Sport & Tourism** [Internet], 14 (2-3), pp. 169-191. Available from: <http://dx.doi.org/10.1080/14775080902965207> [Accessed 06 October 2011].

Preuss, H. (2009) Opportunity costs and efficiency of investments in mega sport events. **Journal of Policy Research in Tourism, Leisure and Events** [Internet], 1 (2), pp. 131-140. Available from: <http://dx.doi.org/10.1080/19407960902992183> [Accessed 06 November 2011].

Raj, R. and Musgrave, J. (2009b) The Economics of Sustainable Events. In Raj, R. and Musgrave, J. eds. **Event Management and Sustainability.** Oxfordshire, CAB International, pp. 56-66.

Saha, D. (2009) Empirical research on local government sustainability efforts in the USA: gaps in the current literature. **Local Environment** [Internet], 14 (1), pp. 17-30. Available from: <http://dx.doi.org/10.1080/13549830802522418> [Accessed 13 November 2011].

Sherman, et al. (2008) **Economics: an introduction to traditional and progressive views.** 7th ed. New York, M.E. Sharpe.

South African Police Service (2011) **Crime Report 2010/2011** [Internet]. Available from: <http://www.saps.gov.za/statistics/reports/crimestats/2011/crime_situation_sa.pdf> [Accessed 02 January 2012].

Steinbrink, M., Haferburg, C. and Ley, A. (2011) Festivalisation and urban renewal in the Global South: socio-spatial consequences of the 2010 FIFA World Cup. **South African Geographical Journal** [Internet], 93 (1), pp. 15-28. Available from: <http://dx.doi.org/10.1080/03736245.2011.567827> [Accessed 04 November 2011].

streetfootballworld (2011) **20 Centres for 2010** [Internet]. Available from: <http://www.streetfootballworld.org/football-for-hope2/20-centres-for-2010> [Accessed 29 December 2011].

Tassiopoulos, D. and Johnson, D. (2009) Social Impacts of Events. In Raj, R. and Musgrave, J. eds. **Event Management and Sustainability.** Oxfordshire, CAB International, pp. 90-99.

Technical Study Group (2010). **2010 FIFA World Cup South Africa – Technical Report and Statistics** [Internet]. Switzerland, FIFA. Available from: <http://www.fifa.com/mm/document/affederation/technicaldevp/01/29/30/95/reportwm2010_web.pdf> [Accessed 14 November 2011].

UNEP - United Nations Environment Programme (2010) **Greening 2010 FIFA World Cup** [Internet]. Available from: <http://www.unep.org/climateneutral/Default.aspx?tabid=496> [Accessed 28 December 2011].

Witt, H. and Loots, L. (2010) Flying the mythical flag of a green and inclusive 2010 FIFA World Cup in KwaZulu-Natal. **Agenda** [Internet], 24 (85), pp. 125-145. Available from: <http://dx.doi.org/10.1080/10130950.2010.9676330> [Accessed 04 November 2011].

World Commission on Environment and Development (1987) **Our Common Future, Chapter 2: Towards Sustainable Development** [Internet], New York, UN Documents: Gathering a Body of Global Agreements. Available from: <http://www.un-documents.net/ocf-02.htm> [Accessed 12 November 2011].

Lightning Source UK Ltd.
Milton Keynes UK
UKHW031255081221
395308UK00007B/816